Tolley's National Insurance Contributions 2009

Pre-Budget Report Supplement

Edited by Jon Golding ATT TEP

Consulting Editor Peter Arrowsmith FCA

LexisNexis®
Tolley

Members of the LexisNexis Group worldwide

United Kingdom	LexisNexis, a Division of Reed Elsevier (UK) Ltd, Halsbury House, 35 Chancery Lane, London, WC2A 1EL, and London House, 20-22 East London Street, Edinburgh EH7 4BQ
Argentina	LexisNexis Argentina, Buenos Aires
Australia	LexisNexis Butterworths, Chatswood, New South Wales
Austria	LexisNexis Verlag ARD Orac GmbH & Co KG, Vienna
Benelux	LexisNexis Benelux, Amsterdam
Canada	LexisNexis Canada, Markham, Ontario
Chile	LexisNexis Chile Ltda, Santiago
China	LexisNexis China, Beijing and Shanghai
France	LexisNexis SA, Paris
Germany	LexisNexis Deutschland GmbH, Munster
Hong Kong	LexisNexis Hong Kong, Hong Kong
India	LexisNexis India, New Delhi
Italy	Giuffrè Editore, Milan
Japan	LexisNexis Japan, Tokyo
Malaysia	Malayan Law Journal Sdn Bhd, Kuala Lumpur
Mexico	LexisNexis Mexico, Mexico
New Zealand	LexisNexis NZ Ltd, Wellington
Poland	Wydawnictwo Prawnicze LexisNexis Sp, Warsaw
Singapore	LexisNexis Singapore, Singapore
South Africa	LexisNexis Butterworths, Durban
USA	LexisNexis, Dayton, Ohio

© Reed Elsevier (UK) Ltd 2009

Published by LexisNexis

A CIP Catalogue record for this book is available from the British Library.

ISBN 9780754537342

Printed and bound in Great Britain by Hobbs the Printers Ltd, Hampshire

Visit LexisNexis at www.lexisnexis.co.uk

About This Pre-Budget Report Statement Supplement

This Pre-Budget Report supplement to the 2009–10 book gives details of changes in the law and practice in connection with National Insurance contributions from the publication of Tolley's National Insurance Contributions 2009–10 up until the Pre-Budget Report Statement on 9 December 2009. It lists the changes in the same order and under the same paragraph headings as the annual publication but will where necessary for completeness be shown next to the original text. This supplement edition also includes the list of updated publications in the Leaflets chapter 43 in full.

Each time Tolley's National Insurance Contributions 2009–10 is used, reference should be made to the material contained in this supplement. The Contents gives a list of all the chapters and paragraphs which have been updated.

TOLLEY

Contents

This supplement contains amendments to the chapters and paragraphs of Tolley's National Insurance Contributions 2009–10 as listed below.

Contents

7   Annual Maximum

Insert the following paragraphs in 7.2 on page 73 after the first paragraph on that page:

There are no provisions enabling the annual maximum to be reduced if the contributor attains pensionable age during the year, thereby ceasing to be liable to primary Class 1 and Class 2 contributions (see **3.7** and **3.12** age exception).

Example

For the whole of 2009–10, Chaffinch is employed by Dunnock in a contracted-out employment at a salary of £3,330 per month. From 6 October 2009 to 5 April 2010, she is also employed by Egret in a not contracted-out employment at a salary of £1,450 per month; and from 1 January 2010, she is also self-employed. The Class 1 primary contributions paid on her earnings from her employed earner's employments are as follows:

	£			£	£
Dunnock	476.00	(monthly ET)	@ Nil%	0.00 × 12 =	0.00
	2,854.00		@ 9.4%	268.28 × 12 =	3,219.36
	3,330.00				3,219.36
Egret	476.00	(monthly ET)	@ Nil%	0.00 × 6 =	0.00
	974.00		@ 11%	107.14 × 6 =	642.84
	1,250.00				642.84
Total Class 1 paid:					3,862.20
Chaffinch also pays:					
Class 2 contributions				£2.40 × 14 =	33.60
					3,895.80

On the face of it, C will not have paid excessive contributions since the notional annual maximum for 2009–10 is £4,279.22. Such a judgement is premature, however. Before the question of any excess can be decided, the primary Class 1 contributions paid at less than standard rate (ie £3,219.36) must be converted to contributions at the appropriate standard rate (ie £3,219.36 × 11/9.4 = £3,767.34) and a fresh total must be arrived at (ie £4,444.38). As this fresh total *exceeds* £4,279.22, excess contributions appear to have been paid. It is therefore necessary to consider Chaffinch's personalised maximum following the numbered steps set out in new *Reg 21* as follows –

Step		£	£
1.	Calculate 53 × (UEL – PT), ie 53 × (£844 – £110)		38,902.00
2.	11% thereof		4,279.22
3.	Earnings from each employment that falls between PT and Upper Earnings Limit: £2,854 × 12 = £34,248 £974 × 6 = £5,844	40,092.00	
4.	Deduct figure in step 1. from 3. (£40,092 – £38,902)	1,190	
5.	If the line above was a positive figure, multiply by 1%		11.90
6.	Earnings from each employment which exceeds UEL	Nil	
7.	Multiply step 6 result by 1%		Nil
8.	Add steps 2, 5, 7 – this gives the personalised annual maximum		4,291.12

1

7 Annual Maximum

The contributions paid do exceed this personalised maximum and, provided the necessary conditions are met, the excess, suitably adjusted, will be repayable (see **55.2** and **55.5** REPAYMENT AND REALLOCATION).

It is important to recognise that the earnings to be included at Step 3 are those which fall between the threshold and the Upper Earnings Limit on a pay-period by pay-period basis, ie the annual total of those earnings which have borne full rate liability (or contracted-out or other equivalents, as the case may be). National Insurance Contributions Office will ascertain this from Box 1c on the Forms P14/P60.

Example

For the whole of 2009–10, Finch is employed by Grebe in a not contracted-out employment at a salary of £3,000 per month, and paid an annual bonus in March of £8,000. She is also employed by Heron in another not contracted-out employment at a salary of £1,800 per month. Neither employment is a directorship. The Class 1 primary contributions paid on her earnings from her employed earner's employments are as follows:

	£			£	£
Grebe	476.00	(monthly ET)	@ Nil%	$0.00 \times 11 =$	0.00
(First 11	2,524.00		@ 11%	$277.64 \times 11 =$	3,054.04
months)					
	3,000.00				3,054.04
(March)	476.00	(monthly ET)	@ Nil%	$0.00 \times 1 =$	0.00
	3,180.00		@ 11%	$349.80 \times 1 =$	349.80
	3,656.00	(monthly UEL)			642.84
	7,344.00		@ 1%	$73.44 \times 1 =$	73.44
	11,000.00				423.24
(Total)					3,477.28
Heron	476.00	(monthly ET)	@ Nil%	$0.00 \times 12 =$	0.00
	1,324.00		@ 11%	$145.64 \times 12 =$	1,747.68
	1,800.00				1,747.68
Total Class 1 paid:					5,224.96

Finch's personalised maximum following the numbered steps set out in new *Reg 21* is as follows:

Step		£	£
1.	Calculate 53 × (UEL – PT), ie 53 × (£844 × £110)		38,902.00
2.	11% thereof		4,279.22
3.	Earnings from each employment that falls between PT and Upper Earnings Limit:		
	£2,524 × 11 = £27,764		
	£3,180 × 1 = £3,180		
	£1,324 × 12 = £15,888	46,832.00	
4.	Deduct figure in step 1. from 3. (£46,832 × £38,902)	7,930	
5.	If the line above was a positive figure, multiply by 1%		79.30

2

Step	£	£
6. Earnings from each employment which exceeds UEL	7,344	
7. Multiply step 6 result by 1%		73.44
8. Add steps 2, 5, 7 – this gives the personalised annual maximum		4,431.96

The contributions paid exceed this personalised maximum and, provided the necessary conditions are met, the excess will be repayable (see **55.2** and **55.5** REPAYMENT AND REALLOCATION).

---

9 Appeals and Reviews

Replace the second sentence in 9.1 on page 98 with the following:

The Tribunals Service (an agency of the Ministry of Justice) is independent of HM Revenue and Customs, who previously controlled listing and other aspects of case management in the former General Commissioners system, which many outside observers have always doubted was sufficiently distanced from HM Revenue and Customs.

Replace third and subsequent paragraphs on page 98 in section 9.1 with the following:

Members of the judiciary will work at the CPC in order to give judicial direction where required and manage cases appropriately. There will also be two full-time, tax-dedicated registrars at the CPC, who will carry out quasi-judicial functions, eg categorise cases received at the CPC into tracks, identify tax cases which are complex (and therefore eligible to enter the costs regime) and bring these to the attention of the judiciary for a decision and liaise with the Upper Tribunal regarding those rare cases which start at that court, or which appeal to it from the First-tier Tax Tribunal.

The route of appeal from the First-tier Tax Tribunal will be to the Upper Tribunal, which is a superior court of record akin to the High Court. Appeal to the Upper Tribunal will be on a point of law only, and with permission of the First-tier Tax Tribunal or the Upper Tribunal. The exception to this will be those extremely rare cases which start in the Upper Tribunal, where onward appeals will be to the Court of Appeal or the Court of Sessions in Scotland.

In all there are six Chambers in the First-tier Tribunal, as follows:

• Social Security and Child Support;

• Health, Education and Social Care;

• War Pensions and Armed Forces Compensation;

• Taxation;

• Land, Property and Housing; and

• General Regulatory.

The first three of the above commenced on 3 November 2008 – the Social Entitlement Chamber handles appeals about state benefits, tax credits and related matters.

There are three Upper Tribunal Chambers, as follows:

• Administrative Appeals;

• Lands; and

• Tax and Chancery (formerly Finance and Tax).

9   Appeals and Reviews

The remainder of this chapter deals with:

- Current procedure for appeals to the Tax Chamber of the Tribunals Service (**9.2** to **9.12**)

- Other decisions heard by the Social Entitlement Chamber of the Tribunals Service (ie those under the *Pension Schemes Act 1993* and those in respect of the awarding of credits and home responsibilities protection) (**9.13**)

Insert the following paragraph after the only paragraph in 9.5 on page 104:

Ordinarily, an appeal will be made first to HM Revenue and Customs who may offer an internal review or who may be asked to undertake a review. The appeal may not be notified to the Tribunal while an internal review is under way.

Replace the first two paragraphs in 9.6 on page 104 with the following paragraphs:

An appeal must be made in writing within 30 days after the date on which the notice of decision was issued. The Guide DAA2 contains a tear-off appeal form (DAA3) which may be used if appealing to HM Revenue and Customs but an appeal made in any format in writing and within the specified 30 days is legally valid.

The notice of appeal must specify the grounds of appeal but on hearing by the Tribunal it may allow additional grounds, not stated in the notice of appeal, to be put forward if satisfied that the omission was neither wilful nor unreasonable. [*SSC(TF)A 1999, s 12(3)*]. An appeal made direct to the Tribunal or notified following an unsuccessful review will be made to the Tribunals Service, Tax, 2nd Floor, 54 Hagley Road, Birmingham B16 8PE using Form TaxApp1 (and thereafter all administration is undertaken by the Tribunals Service). See form below.

However, a statutory review procedure was introduced from 1 April 2009 and is a statutory right for appellants, but not compulsory. This internal review by HM Revenue and Customs will, in NIC cases, usually be carried out by someone in the Regional Appeals Unit but the reviewing officer cannot be the advocate at the appeal hearing on the same case. Even if outside the Regional Appeals Unit, the review will always be carried out by someone outside the direct line management of the case-worker or decision-maker.

Where the appellant requests a review, HM Revenue and Customs must issue a letter within 30 days which then constitutes the start of the review period. Where HM Revenue and Customs itself offers a review, the appellant has 30 days to either accept the review offer or notify the appeal to the Tribunal. The appellant's letter accepting the review offer constitutes the start of the review period.

Except in 2009 transitional cases, the review period is 45 days unless HM Revenue and Customs requests a longer period. If HM Revenue and Customs requests a longer period and the appellant is minded not to allow a longer period, the original decision stands and must be either accepted or the appeal notified to the Tribunal.

Replace the last paragraph in 9.6 on page 110 with the following paragraph:

The Board have the power to make regulations, with the concurrence of the Lord Chancellor and the Lord Advocate, in respect of contributions, Statutory Sick Pay, Statutory Maternity Pay, Statutory Paternity Pay or Statutory Adoption Pay appeals and may also make regulations regarding matters arising pending a decision of an officer under *s 8*, pending the determination by the Tax Tribunal, out of the variation of a decision or out of the superseding of a decision. [*SSC(TF)A 1999, s 13* as amended by *Revenue and Customs Appeals Order 2009, SI 2009/ 777, Reg 3*; *SSC(TF)A 1999, s 14*]

Replace the title in 9.10 on page 111 with the following:

9.10   Determination by First-tier Tax Tribunal

Replace the first sentence in 9.11 on page 111 with the following:

Appellants may, before an appeal is heard by the First-tier Tax Tribunal of the Tribunals Service, come to an agreement with an officer of the Board that the decision under appeal should be treated as

Replace the first sentence in 9.12 on page 112 with the following:

9.12   Dissatisfaction with First-tier Tax Tribunal's determination

If HM Revenue and Customs, the appellant or another party to the proceedings think that the First-tier Tax Tribunal's decision is wrong on a point of law, then an appeal may be made to the Tax and Chancery Chamber of the Upper Tribunal (the Finance and Tax Chamber was renamed with effect from 1 September 2009 by the *First-tier Tribunal and Upper Tribunal (Chambers) (Amendment No 3) Order 2009, SI 2009/1590*). That is unless it is classed as an excluded decision either on the face of the Act or in any order made by the Lord Chancellor. [*Tribunals, Courts and Enforcement Act 2007, s 11*].

12   Arrears of Contributions

Add the following paragraph after the last paragraph in 12.6 on page 146:

In *HMRC v Benchdollar Ltd & Others Ch D [2009] EWHC 1310 (Ch)* HMRC issued determinations that NIC was chargeable on the payments in question being remuneration paid as benefits in kind thereby avoiding NICs. The employers appealed. However, several of these appeals took a very long time to resolve, and HMRC became concerned that they might be unable to collect the contributions because of the six-year time limit laid down by *Limitation Act 1980, s 9*. HMRC also wished to avoid the cost of beginning county court proceedings to recover the contributions, knowing that the recovery proceedings would have to be adjourned pending the outcome of the employers' appeals to the Commissioners. HMRC therefore asked the employers to give a formal acknowledgement of HMRC's claims, without making any admission of liability. However, in August 2001, HMRC received legal advice that this procedure did not have the desired effect of circumventing the statutory time limit laid down by *Limitation Act 1980, s 9*. The substantive appeals were subsequently determined in favour of HMRC, but the employers declined to pay the contributions, and HMRC began proceedings in the Newcastle-upon-Tyne county court. The employers defended the proceedings, contending that the effect of *Limitation Act 1980, s 9* was that they had been begun outside the statutory time limit. The county court referred the case to the Chancery Division for rulings on the interpretation of *Limitation Act 1980, s 9*. Briggs J reviewed the relevant correspondence in detail and held that 'the combination of a detrimental reliance by HMRC, coupled with the obtaining by the relevant employers of the anticipated benefit of HMRC's reliance upon the shared assumption, is sufficient to render it unfair and unjust for those employers now to advance a limitation defence in relation to NICs arising out of the 1994/95 tax year. In short, in relation to NICs for that tax year, the employers are estopped by convention from asserting the ineffectiveness of the acknowledgements or part payments.' However, HMRC had become aware of the ineffectiveness of their proposed procedure by August 2001. Therefore, with regard to claims that became statute-barred after September 2001, HMRC should have taken alternative steps to protect its position. By failing to do so, HMRC was 'the author of its own misfortune' and employers facing such claims were entitled to 'assert a limitation defence to those claims, arising out of HMRC's decision not to protect them once aware of the true legal position'.

19   Class 3 Contributions: Voluntary

Insert the following sentence at the end of the fourth paragraph in 19.2 on page 259:

See *I Osborne v HMRC (and related appeals) [2009] UKFTT 421 (TC00190)*.

21   Collection

Replace the last paragraph in 21.5 on page 283 and the first paragraph on page 284 with the following

As part of measures to encourage employers to file end of year returns electronically there are financial incentives for those with less than 50 employees from 2008–09 of £75 (non-taxable if the electronic filing is complete, accurate and successful. Similar but larger incentives were made available for the previous four years. This will be compulsory for the year 2009–10 (ie May 2010 filing date) onwards when the financial incentive ceases to exist (though there are a few exceptions – see below) and it should be noted that the announcement on Budget day 2007 of the deferral of requirements to submit Forms P45 and P46 electronically extends only to those particular proposals and not to the P35/P14 e-filing plans. For employers employing between 50 and 249 employees the first compulsory filing year was 2005–06 (ie May 2006) and employers with over 249 employees had to file electronically for 2004–05 (ie May 2005). [*Social Security (Contributions) Regulations 2001, Reg 90N*, inserted by *Social Security (Contributions, Categorisation of Earners and Intermediaries) (Amendment) Regulations 2004, SI 2004/770, Reg 23*]. There is a separate penalty of up to £3,000 per annum per PAYE scheme where an employer is required to 'e-file' but fails to do so either at all or if made otherwise than electronically and this is in addition the existing late filing penalty. [*Social Security (Contributions) Regulations 2001, Reg 90P*, inserted by *Social Security (Contributions, Categorisation of Earners and Intermediaries) (Amendment) Regulations 2004, SI 2004/770, Reg 23* and amended by *Social Security (Contributions) (Amendment No. 4) Regs 2009, SI 2009/2028, Reg 8*]. See IR Press Release IR 90/03, 3 November 2003 and Working Together, Issue 12 page 4, Issue 22 page 1.

The electronic filing requirement will not apply to any PAYE scheme which ceases to pay any employees during 2009/10 **and** the return is filed on paper **before** 6 April 2010. Beyond this the following employers will also be able to claim exemption from the requirement to file online:

•   religious groups whose beliefs are incompatible with using electronic communications;

•   those operating 'Simplified PAYE Schemes' – these are for domestic or personal employees whose taxable earnings do not exceed – currently – £160 per week/£700 per month; and

•   care and support employers.

The latter group means an individual who employs a person to provide domestic or personal services at the employer's home where:

•   the employee's services are provided to the employer or a member of the employer's family; and

•   the person receiving the services suffers from a physical or mental disability, or is elderly or infirm.

Domestic PAYE schemes seeking exemption from electronic filing should not ever have received an efiling incentive; care and support employers seeking exemption from electronic filing should not have received an efiling incentive in the previous three years (thus making the stipulation redundant in respect of 2011/12 returns onwards). [*Social Security (Contributions) (Amendment No. 4) Regulations 2009, SI 2009/2028* and *Income Tax (Pay As You Earn) (Amendment No. 2) Regulations 2009, SI 2009/2029*].

It is important to note that all electronic returns must meet a Quality Standard (QS) and HM Revenue and Customs strongly recommend that QS is built into day to day payroll software. [*Social Security (Contributions) Regulations 2001, Reg 90O*, inserted by *Social Security (Contributions, Categorisation of Earners and Intermediaries) (Amendment) Regulations 2004,*

SI 2004/770, Reg 23]. In this connection, the exacting standards are available on the website at http://www.hmrc.gov.uk/ebu/qual_stand.htm. Commercially marketed software with the *Payroll Standard* accreditation will meet the QS requirements. Every PAYE scheme should have received an advisory letter in late 2003 giving the employer the chance to get help or sign up for on-line filing and specifying the size as measured by HM Revenue and Customs over the last weekend of October 2003. Such head-count was definitive for 2004–05 filing, regardless of subsequent changes in circumstances. A further such letter was sent in November 2004 regarding 2005–06 obligations and so on. Employers are able to appeal if they think that HM Revenue and Customs has placed them in the wrong category for on-line filing deadlines. Employees excluded from the count for on-line filing will be those earning below the Lower Earnings Limit (LEL) and those with earnings that should be shown on the P38A. [*The Income Tax (Pay As You Earn) Regulations 2003, SI 2003/2682, Regs 205–210*]. The *Finance Act 2007* added further powers to the e-filing requirements of large businesses in the form of extending *FA 2003, s 204* to require the making of payments electronically across all HMRC taxes and duties in due course. [*FA 2003, s 204* as amended by *FA 2007, s 94*].

Replace the fourth paragraph in 21.8 on page 292 with the following:

The *Finance Act 2007, Sch 24* set the framework for a new penalty regime applying a percentage loading to the tax and NICs due figure as a result of correcting an inaccuracy or resulting in an assessment for non-disclosure. These arrangements first apply to Class 1 National Insurance in respect of the 2008–09 P35s and to Class 4 in respect of the 2008-09 self-assessment returns. However, the old penalty regime described above will still apply for some time to come in the case of older returns.

25   Crown Servants and Diplomatic Agents

Insert the following sentence in 25.6 in place of the last two sentences in the fourth paragraph on page 355:

Any question which arises as to whether a person is entitled to privilege or immunity is to be settled conclusively by a certificate issued by or under the authority of the Secretary of State (ie, Home Secretary). See *Jimenez v CIR [2004] STC SCD 371 Sp C 419*. [*DPA 1964, s 4*].

29   Earnings from employment: General

Insert the following case after the first sentence of the second paragraph in the Example on page 401 in 29.19:

See *North Yorkshire Police and Mrs Deborah Wade v HMRC [2009] (TC00186)*.

30   Earnings from employment: Expenses

Insert the following Table in place of the Tables shown in paragraph 30.18 on pages 445 to 447:

HM Revenue and Customs guideline rates for NICs

	Petrol			Diesel		LPG		
From	*Up to 1400cc*	*1401 to 2000cc*	*Over 2000cc*	*Up to 2000cc*	*Over 2000cc*	*Up to 1400cc*	*1401 to 2000cc*	*Over 2000cc*
1 Dec 2009	11p	14p	20p	11p	14p	7p	8p	12p
1 Jul 2009	10p	12p	18p	10p	13p	7p	8p	12p
1 Jan 2009	10p	12p	17p	11p	14p	7p	9p	12p
1 Jul 2008	12p	15p	21p	13p	17p	7p	9p	13p
1 Jan 2008	11p	13p	19p	11p	14p	7p	8p	11p

31　Earnings from employment: Readily convertible assets, etc

| From | Petrol | | | Diesel | | LPG | | |
	Up to 1400cc	1401 to 2000cc	Over 2000cc	Up to 2000cc	Over 2000cc	Up to 1400cc	1401 to 2000cc	Over 2000c
1 Aug 2007	10p	13p	18p	10p	13p	6p	8p	10p
1 Feb 2007	9p	11p	16p	9p	12p	6p	7p	10p
1 Jul 2006	11p	13p	18p	10p	14p	7p	8p	11p
1 Jul 2005	10p	12p	16p	9p	13p	7p	8p	10p
6 Apr 2004	10p	12p	14p	9p	12p	7p	8p	10p
6 Apr 2002	10p	12p	14p	9p	12p	6p	7p	9p

Mileage allowances which are not related to actual business mileage are merely round sum allowances (see **30.13** above). (CWG2 (2009) page 90).

Insert the following Table in place of the Table shown in paragraph 30.19 on page 449:

Inland Revenue authorised rates for NICs

Year	Up to 1000cc	1001 to 1500cc	1501 to 2000cc	Over 2000cc
2001–02	40p	40p	45p	63p
2000–01	28p	35p	45p	63p
1999–2000	28p	35p	45p	63p
1998–99	28p	35p	45p	63p

31　Earnings from employment: Readily convertible assets, etc

Replace the second paragraph in 31.11 on page 465 with the following:

In the case of the EMI there is individual limit of £120,000. The company must have less than 250 employees and less than £30 million gross assets. There is no limit on the exercise period which can therefore be very short. An advantage of EMI over unapproved options is that HM Revenue and Customs will agree market values in advance of granting the options. Provided the exercise price is no lower than market value there will not generally be a charge to income tax or Class 1 National Insurance on the exercise. If the exercise price is below market value then income tax will be payable on exercise and if the shares are readily convertible assets, the tax will in the form of PAYE and there will be Class 1 National Insurance contributions. Where EMI options are granted at a discount or there is a disqualifying event an income tax charge and almost certainly a Class 1 National Insurance charge will arise when the options are exercised. No charges arise on grant. EMI is attractive to companies as they can obtain corporation tax relief on the value of shares at exercise less sums paid and if granted at market value there will be neither income tax nor National Insurance charges on exercise, the gain falling only within the capital gains tax regime.

In 31.20 replace the last paragraph on page 471 and the first paragraph on page 472 with the following:

The UK investment exchanges recognised under the *Financial Services and Markets Act 2000, s 287* as at 16 November 2009 are:

• 　　EDX London Ltd

• 　　ICE Futures Europe

• 　　LIFFE Administration and Management (London International Financial Futures Exchange

- London Stock Exchange plc
- PLUS Markets plc
- The London Metal Exchange Ltd

The overseas investment exchanges recognised under the *Financial Services and Markets Act 2000, s 287* by the Treasury as at 16 November 2009 are:

- Cantor Financial Futures Exchange (CFEE)
- Chicago Board of Trade (CBOT)
- EUREX Zurich
- ICE Futures US, Inc
- National Association of Securities Dealers Automated Quotations (NASDAQ)
- New York Mercantile Exchange (NYMEX Inc.)
- SIX Swiss Exchange AG
- Sydney Futures Exchange Ltd (SFE)
- The Chicago Mercantile Exchange (CME)

35   Enforcement

Replace the first three paragraphs of 35.4 on pages 517 and 518 with the following:

From 1 April 2009 the provisions of *Finance Act 2008, Schedule 36* apply to National Insurance contributions as they do to tax.

[*Social Security Contributions and Benefits Act 1992, s 110ZA*, as substituted by *Finance Act 2008, Schedule 36, para 84*]

As regards employers, the records inspected under the *Finance Act 2008, Schedule 36* regime will be those required to be maintained under *Social Security (Contributions) Regulations 2001, SI 2001/1004, Sch 4 para 26(1)*, as amended by *Social Security (Contributions) (Amendment No 3) Regulations 2009, SI 2009/600, Reg 8(4)*.

An employer must keep, in addition to those documents required to be submitted to HM Revenue and Customs, all Class 1 contribution records for not less than three years after the end of the tax year to which they relate and, in the case of Class 1A and Class 1B, documents or records relating to the amount payable for a like period.

'Contribution records' means wages sheets, deductions working sheets, and other documents or records relating to the calculation of payment of earnings and the amount of contributions payable on those earnings as well as documents, records and 'any information' about the amounts of Class 1A and/or Class 1B payable by the employer. [*Social Security (Contributions) Regulations 2001, SI 2001/1004, Sch 4 para 26(40*, as amended by *Social Security (Contributions) (Amendment No 3) Regulations 2009, SI 2009/600, Reg 8(4)*].

The contribution records or other documents and records may be kept in any format [*Social Security (Contributions) Regulations 2001, SI 2001/1004, Sch 4 para 26(2)* as amended by *Social Security (Contributions) (Amendment No 3) Regulations 2009, SI 2009/600, Reg 8(4)*].

Prior to April 2009, the obligations employers and other contributors were contained wholly within the social security legislation. There was a duty to give an officer information when he reasonably required it.

42   Late-Paid Contributions

Anyone

(a)   who is the occupier of premises liable to inspection (see **35.2** above);

(b)   who is, or has been, employing another;

(c)   who is carrying on an employment agency or similar business;

(d)   who is a servant or agent of any person falling within (a) to (c) above;

(e)   who is, or has been, liable to pay contributions; or

(f)   who is, or has been, a trustee or manager of a personal or occupational pension scheme

must furnish an officer with all such information, and produce for his inspection all such documents, as he might reasonably require for the purpose of ascertaining whether any contributions due were payable, had been payable, or had been duly paid, by, or in respect of any person. This included all wages sheets, deduction working sheets and other documents and records relating to the calculation of earnings, earnings-related contributions and Class 1A contributions. An officer may decide that he/she needs to check information about working practices of the company to see if it has reached the correct view on the application of the IR 35 legislation when the form P35 was filed. This may prove difficult as evidenced in *Tilbury Consulting Ltd v Gittins [2004] STC SCD 1 Sp C379*. [*Social Security (Contributions) Regulations 2001, SI 2001/1004, Sch 4 para 26(1)*; *The Income Tax (Pay As You Earn) Regulations 2003, SI 2003/2682, Reg 97(1)(2)*].

Any documents reasonably required were to be produced at the prescribed place. [*Social Security (Contributions) Regulations 2001, SI 2001/1004, Sch 4 para 26(1)*]. This means such place in Great Britain as the employer and the officer may agree upon. If no agreement is reached, they must be produced at the place in Great Britain at which they are normally kept or, if there is no such place, at the employer's principal place of business in Great Britain. [*Former Social Security (Contributions) Regulations 2001, SI 2001/1004, Sch 4 para 26(2)*]. The officer was empowered to take copies of, or make extracts from, any documents produced to him and, if it appears to him to be necessary, at a reasonable time and for a reasonable period to take away any such document, providing a receipt to the employer. If any of the documents removed is reasonably required for the conduct of the business, the officer must provide a copy, free of charge, within seven days of its being taken away. [*Former Social Security (Contributions) Regulations 2001, SI 2001/1004, Sch 4 para 26(3)*; *The Income Tax (Pay As You Earn) Regulations 2003, SI 2003/2682, Reg 97(3)(4)(5)*].

42   Late-Paid Contributions

Insert the following paragraph before the penultimate paragraph on page 597 in 42.9:

Further, the Autumn 2009 floods in certain parts of the UK, any businesses that were affected can agreeing a revised payment schedule for tax or NICs as a result of any serious financial difficulties encountered because of the floods. There is a HMRC number for assistance for those affected being 08453 000157 and it is available seven days a week, 8am to 8pm.

43   Leaflets and Forms

Insert on pages 599 to 605 in place of the paragraphs in 43.2 to 43.5:

43.2   Leaflets

HM Revenue and Customs, together with the DWP and its agencies, produce various leaflets, many of which are specifically aimed at employers (ie manuals, tables and fact cards), and these are listed below.

Leaflets regarding National Insurance Contributions are issued by HM Revenue and Customs (except for SA series leaflets, which are issued by the DWP). It should be noted that HM Revenue and Customs has withdrawn a number of NIC leaflets during 2005 and 2006. See **43.3** for application forms formerly contained in now withdrawn leaflets. Those leaflets that remain available can be obtained from

* local HM Revenue and Customs (NIC) offices

+ only from the HM Revenue and Customs website

++ HMRC (Residency), NICO, Longbenton, NEWCASTLE UPON TYNE NE98 1ZZ or Department for Work and Pensions, Pensions and Overseas Benefits Directorate, Customer Service Unit, Room TC 109, NEWCASTLE UPON TYNE NE98 1BA.

Employers Orderline (08457 646 646)

DWP only from http://www.dwp.gov.uk/lifeevent/benefits/social_security_agreements.asp

In addition, many of the leaflets for employers are on the Employer's CD-ROM (obtainable from the Employers Orderline 08457 646 646 and http://www.hmrc.gov.uk/employers/emp-form.htm)

National Insurance Leaflets

Number		Date	Name
	AO 1	2009	The Adjudicator's Office for complaints about HM Revenue and Customs and the Valuation Office Agency
+	CA 14	Jun 02	Termination of Contracted-out Employment Manual for Salary Related Pension Schemes and Salary Related Parts of Mixed Benefits Schemes
+	CA 14A	Apr 02	Termination of Contracted-out Employment Manual for Money Purchase Pension Schemes and Money Purchase Parts of Mixed Benefits Schemes
+	CA 14C	May 07	Contracted-out Guidance for Salary Related Pension Schemes and Salary Related Overseas Schemes
+	CA 14D	May 07	Contracted-out Guidance for Money Purchase Pension Schemes and Money Purchase Overseas Schemes
+	CA 14E	May 07	Contracted-out Guidance for Mixed Benefit Pension Schemes and Mixed Benefit Overseas Schemes
+	CA 14F	Apr 03	Technical Guidance on Contracted-Out Decision Making and Appeals
+	CA 15	Feb 05	Cessation of Contracted-out Pension Schemes Manual
+	CA 16	Nov 08	Appropriate Personal Pension Scheme Manual – Procedural Guidance
+	CA 16A	May 07	Appropriate Personal Pension Scheme Manual – Guidance for Scheme Managers
+	CA 17	Nov 08	Employee's guide to minimum contributions
+	CA 19	Apr 03	Using the Accrued GMP Liability Service
+	CA 20	Mar 03	Using the Contracted-out Contributions/ Earnings Information Service

43 Leaflets and Forms

	Number	Date	Name
+	CA 21	Jul 04	Using the National Insurance Number/Date of Birth Checking Service
+	CA 22	Oct 02	Contracted-out Data Transactions using Magnetic Media
#	CA 33	Apr 09	Class 1A National Insurance contributions on Car and Fuel Benefits – A guide for employers
*	CA 37	Apr 09	Simplified Deductions Scheme for employers
#	CA 38	Apr 09	Not contracted-out Tables (Tables A, J)
#	CA 39	Apr 09	Contracted-out contributions for employers with Contracted-out Salary Related Schemes (Tables D, E, L)
#	CA 40	Apr 09	Employee only contributions tables for employers or employees authorised to pay their own contributions
#	CA 41	Apr 09	Not contracted-out Tables (Tables B and C)
+	CA 42	Apr 09	Foreign-Going Mariner's and Deep Sea Fisherman's contributions for employers
#	CA 43	Apr 09	Contracted-out contributions and minimum payments for employers with contracted-out Money Purchase Schemes (Tables F, G, S)
#	CA 44	Dec 08	National Insurance for Company Directors (Employer Manual)
+	CA 84	Oct 02	Stakeholder Pension Scheme Manual – Procedural Guidance
+	CA 85	May 03	Contracted-out Stakeholder Pension Scheme Manual
*	CA 89	Sep 07	Payroll Cleansing. A free service offered by HMRC
+	C/FS	Apr 07	Complaints and putting things right
+	CF 411		Home Responsibilities Protection
#	CWG 2	Dec 08	Employer Further Guide to PAYE and NICs
#	CWG 5	Dec 08	Class 1A National Insurance contributions on benefits in kind – A guide for employers
#	E 10	Dec 08	Employer Help Book. Finishing the tax year up to 5 April 2009
#	E 11	Dec 08	Employer Help Book. Starting the tax year from 6 April 2009
#	E 12	Dec 08	Employer Help Book. PAYE and NICs rates and limits for 2009–10
#	E 13	Dec 08	Employer Help Book. Day-to-day payroll
#	E 14	Dec 08	Employer Help Book for Statutory Sick Pay
#	E 15	Dec 08	Employer Help Book for Statutory Maternity Pay
#	E 16	Dec 08	Employer Help Book for Statutory Adoption Pay
+	E 18	Sep 08	How you can help your employees with childcare

	Number	Date	Name
#	E 19	Dec 08	Employer Help Book for Statutory Paternity Pay
+	E 24	2009	Tips, Gratuities, Service Charges and troncs. A guide to Income Tax, National Insurance contributions, National Minimum Wage issues, and VAT
+	EC/FS1	Feb 09	Employers and contractors – reviewing your records
+	EC/FS2	Feb 09	Large employers and contractors – reviewing your records
+	EC/FS3	Feb 09	Compliance checks – what happens during and at the end of a check
+	EC/FS4	Feb 09	Compliance checks – types of penalty
+	EC/FS5	Feb 09	Employers and contractors compliance checks – your obligations
+	ES/FS1	Jun 08	Employed or self-employed for tax and National Insurance contributions
+	ES/FS2	Aug 08	Are your workers employed or self-employed for tax and National Insurance contributions
+	HMRC 1	Mar 09	HM Revenue & Customs decisions – what to do if you disagree
*	IR 115	Nov 08	Income tax, National Insurance contributions and childcare
*	IR 121	Jul 06	Approaching retirement A guide to tax and National Insurance contributions
++	NI 38	Sep 09	Social Security abroad
	DWPSA 4		Social security agreement between the United Kingdom and Jersey and Guernsey
	DWPSA 8		Social security agreement between the United Kingdom and New Zealand
	DWPSA 14		Social security agreement between United Kingdom and Israel
	DWPSA 17		Social security agreement between United Kingdom and the Republics of the former Yugoslavia
	DWPSA 20		Social security agreement between the United Kingdom and Canada
	DWPSA 22		Social security agreement between the United Kingdom and Turkey
	DWPSA 23		Social security agreement between United Kingdom and Bermuda
	DWPSA 27		Social security agreement between United Kingdom and Jamaica
	DWPSA 29		Your social security insurance, benefits and healthcare rights in the European Community

43 Leaflets and Forms

Number	Date	Name
DWPSA 33		Social security agreement between the United Kingdom and United States of America
DWPSA 38		Social security agreement between United Kingdom and Mauritius
DWPSA 42		Social security agreement between the United Kingdom and Philippines
DWPSA 43		Social security agreement between the United Kingdom and Barbados
* SE 1	May 07	Are you thinking of working for yourself?

Other social security leaflets are available from local social security offices, except where indicated

* only available from Child Support Literature Line, Room 164E, DSS Longbenton, NEWCASTLE UPON TYNE NE98 1YX (phone 08457 133133 fax 0191 2254572)

+ only available from Department of Health, PO Box 777, LONDON SE1 6XH

++ Pensions Guide, Freepost RLXH-JUEU-GZCH, NORTHAMPTON NN3 6DF (phone 08457 31 32 33, textphone 08456 040210)

** Phone 08701 555455; email: dh@prolog.uk.com

only available from Service Personnel & Veterans Agency Distribution Unit, Room 8102, Norcross, Thornton-Cleveleys FY5 3WP and http://www.veterans-uk.info/publications/leaflets.html

Number	Date	Name
AAA5DCS	Jan 06	Attendance Allowance
BF 225	Nov 08	State Pension dependants allowance
BR19L	Apr 08	State Pension forecast
BRA5DWP	Aug 09	Social Security Benefit Rates
CAA5DCS	May 09	Carer's Allowance
CPF 1	Jun 08	Take part in combined pension forecasts
CPF 2	Apr 07	A guide to combined pension forecasts
CPF 3	Apr 07	Combined pension forecasts – technical guide
CPF 4	Apr 08	Registration notes and CPF form
CPF 5	Jul 09	Your pension statement
* CSA 2001	Dec 05	Child Support for parents who live apart
* CSA 2002	May 01	Changes in child maintenance. Advice to Employers
* CSL 301	Apr 07	What is child maintenance and how does it affect me?
* CSL 302	Apr 07	How do I get child maintenance if I'm on benefits?
* CSL 303	Aug 07	How is child maintenance worked out?
* CSL 304	Apr 07	What happens if someone denies they are the parent of a child?
* CSL 305	Apr 07	How do I pay child maintenance?

14

	Number	Date	Name
*	CSL 306	Apr 07	What action can the Child Support Agency take if parents don't pay?
*	CSL 307	Apr 07	How can I appeal against a child maintenance decision?
*	CSL 308	Apr 07	How do I complain about the service I get from the Child Support Agency?
*	CSL 309	Apr 07	How do I apply for child maintenance? For children living in Scotland
*	CSL 310	Apr 07	Why is the Child Support Agency changing my child maintenance and how will it be different?
*	CSL 311	Apr 07	How does the Child Support Agency use and store information?
*	CSL 312	Dec 05	Child Support: a technical guide
*	CSL 313	Apr 07	What is my role in helping my employees pay child maintenance?
*	CSL 314	Apr 07	How will I receive child maintenance?
	DLAA5DCS	Jan 06	Disability Living Allowance
	DLACA5DCS	Jan 06	Disability Living Allowance for children
	DWP1001	Oct 08	Employment and Support Allowance
	DWP1002	May 08	Jobseekers Allowance
	DWP1003	Mar 08	Income Support
	DWP1004	Sep 09	Industrial Injuries Disablement Benefit
	DWP1005	Oct 08	Bereavement Benefits
	DWP1006	May 08	National Insurance
	DWP1007	May 08	Social Fund
	DWP1008	Feb 08	Workpath
	DWP1015	Oct 08	Help with housing costs
	DWP1016	Apr 09	Help with job interviews
	DWP1017	Mar 08	Finding a job
	DWP1019	Oct 08	Permitted Work
	DWP1020	Apr 09	Statutory Sick Pay
	DWP1021	Apr 09	The Disability Symbol and the Disability Discrimination Act
	DWP1023	Jun 08	Volunteering while receiving benefits
	DWP1024	Mar 09	Our service standards
	DWP1025	Dec 08	Tell us what you think
	DWP1026	Jul 08	Help if you are ill or disabled
	DWP1027	Jan 09	What to do after a death (in England and Wales)
	DWP1028	May 09	New Deal – extra support to find work

15

43 Leaflets and Forms

	Number	Date	Name
	DWP1029	May 08	Going into hospital
	DWP1030	Oct 08	A guide for parents
	DWP1031	Oct 08	Having a baby
	GL 22	Jun 08	Tell us how to improve our service
	GL 24DWP	Feb 09	If you think our decision is wrong
+	HC 11	Apr 09	Help with health costs
+	HC 12	Apr 09	A quick guide to help with health costs including charges and optical voucher values
#	Leaflet 1	Apr 09	Notes about the War Disablement Pension and War Widows or Widowers Pension
#	Leaflet 2	Nov 08	Notes for people getting a War Pension living in the United Kingdom
#	Leaflet 3	Nov 08	Notes for people getting a War Pension living overseas
#	Leaflet 4	Nov 08	Notes about rejected claims for War Disablement and War Widows or Widowers pensions living in the United Kingdom
#	Leaflet 5	Nov 08	Notes about rejected claims for War Disablement and War Widows or Widowers pensions living overseas
#	Leaflet 6	Nov 08	Notes for War Pensioners and War Widows or Widower pensioners going abroad
#	Leaflet 7	Dec 08	Notes for Ex-Far East and Korean Prisoners of War
#	Leaflet 9	Apr 09	Rates of War Pensions and allowances 2009–2010
#	Leaflet 10	Dec 08	Notes about War Pension claims for deafness
#	Leaflet 11	Apr 08	How we decide who receives a War Disablement Pension
#	Leaflet 12	Apr 03	Ex-Gratia payment for British troops who were held prisoner by the Japanese during World War Two
#	Leaflet 13	2008	Can we help? Getting your complaint heard
#	Leaflet 14	Jun 04	A Guide To Direct Payment
	NP 46	Jun 08	A guide to State Pensions
++	OVER50	Apr 06	Are you over 50? A practical guide to advice, support and services across government
	PC1L	Nov 09	Pension Credit: Do I qualify and how much could I get?
	PG1	Oct 07	Pensioners' guide
++	PM 2	Feb 08	State pensions. Your guide
++	PM 2	Feb 08	Pensions for women
++	PM 7	Jan 08	Contracted-out pensions. Your guide
	PME 1	Nov 05	Stakeholder pensions. A guide for employers

	Number	Date	Name
	PSCUST1	Jun 08	The Pension Service Customer Charter
	PTB 1	Sep 09	Pensions: the basics. A guide from the Government
	SERPSL 1	Dec 07	Inheritance of SERPS. Important information for married people
++	SPD 1	May 08	Your State Pension Choice – Pension now or extra pension later. A guide to State Pension Deferral
++	SPD 2	Jul 09	Deferring your State Pension
	SPE 01	Jan 09	State pension changes and what they mean for you
**	T 7.1	May 06	Health advice for Travellers
	VACDPA5DCS	Jun 09	Vaccine Damage Payments
	WFPL 1	Jul 09	Guide to Winter Fuel Payments 2009/10
#	WPA GV1	Mar 03	Claims for War Pensions Notes for Gulf Veterans
#	WPWS-1		War Pensioners' Welfare Service Serving Those Who Served

43.3   Application forms

A number of leaflets that HM Revenue and Customs has completely withdrawn in 2005 and 2006 (ie it is not simply the case that they are only available on the internet) contained important application/claim forms. These can now be downloaded from http://www.hmrc.gov.uk/leaflets/obsolete.htm and are as follows

Former leaflet	Form	Form title
CA 02	CF 10	Application for exception for liability for Class 2 contributions (small earnings exception)
CA 08	CA 5603	To pay voluntary National Insurance contributions
CA 09	CF 9A	National Insurance contributions for widows or widowers
CA 13	CF 9	Married woman application for a certificate of election or to change to full liability
CA 72	CA 72A	Application for deferment of payment of Class 1 contributions
CA 72	CA 72B	Application for deferment of payment of Class 2 and Class 4 contributions

CA 72A and CA 72B forms in relation to deferment applications (including some forms for older years) are obtainable from http://www.hmrc.gov.uk/nic/deferment.htm and http://www.hmrc.gov.uk/individuals/fgcat-deferment.shtml

Other forms (though some are duplicated from the above list) can be downloaded from http://www.hmrc.gov.uk/nic/forms.htm as follows

Form	Form title
CA 1586	National Insurance Services to Pension Industry Forms – list and order form
CA 5601	Application to pay Class 2 National Insurance contributions by Direct Debit
CA 5603	To pay voluntary National Insurance contributions
CA 6855	Employers application for National Insurance Number Trace

43   Leaflets and Forms

Form	Form title
CA 72A	Application for deferment of payment of Class 1 contributions
CA 72B	Application for deferment of payment of Class 2 and Class 4 contributions
CA 82	If you think our decision is wrong
CF 9	Married woman application for a certificate of election or to change to full liability
CF 9A	National Insurance contributions for widows or widowers
CF 411	Home Responsibilities Protection (HRP) – application form
CF 411 Notes	Home Responsibilities Protection (HRP) – notes

CA 72A and CA 72B forms in relation to deferment applications (including some forms for older years) are obtainable from http://www.hmrc.gov.uk/nic/deferment.htm and http://www.hmrc.gov.uk/individuals/fgcat-deferment.shtml

Forms in connection with international matters can be downloaded from http://www.hmrc.gov.uk/cnr/osc.htm#6 as follows

Form	Form title
CA 3638	National Insurance Contributions – How you can get a Retirement Pension Forecast
CA 3821	National Insurance Contributions – For employers whose employees are going to work in a European Economic Area (EEA)/Reciprocal Agreement Country
CA 3822	National Insurance Contributions – Application for a certificate of continuing UK liability, including form E101 – when employees are going to work abroad
CA 3837	National Insurance Contributions – Application for form E101 when a self-employed person goes to work in the European Economic Area (EEA)
CA 8421	Application for form E101 when an employee is employed in two or more countries of the EEA
CA 8421A	Application for E101/E106 when an International Transport Worker is employed in two or more countries of the EEA
CA 8450	Application for certificate of continuing liability for groups of performers and crew (employed persons)
CA 8451	Application for certificate of continuing liability for groups of performers and crew (self-employed persons)
CA 8454	Application for certificate E106 or E109

43.4   HM Revenue and Customs Tax Bulletin

The HMRC Tax Bulletin was published every other month until December 2006. From April 1999 it contained relevant National Insurance material. This was in place of the CA 'National Insurance News', the final issue of which was No 12, Winter 1998–99. All Tax Bulletins can be viewed on the HMRC website at http://www.hmrc.gov.uk/bulletins/ and relevant extracts from both CA National Insurance News and Tax Bulletins can be found in previous editions of this work at Chapter 61.

43.5   Contributors' Charter

The former Inland Revenue booklet CA47 'Charter for National Insurance contributors' was withdrawn in mid-2004 and replaced by HMRC Code of Practice 1 – leaflet COP 1. That was in turn replaced in May 2007 by the new fact sheet C/FS Complaints and putting things right (though its stated issue date is April 2007).

A new HM Revenue and Customs Customer Charter came into effect on 11 November 2009 and has legal recognition [*Finance Act 2009, s 91*].

46   Ministers of Religion

Replace the first paragraph in 46.3 on pages 621 and 622 with the following:

HM Revenue and Customs regards reimbursements to ministers of religion for household expenses (eg, heating and lighting, cleaning) as payments towards expenses actually incurred in the employment (*ITEPA 2003, ss 290A, 290B, 351*). In so doing it is recognised that ministers of religion pursue a pastoral vocation which encompasses their whole way of life and of which their families form an integral part and also that they may be required to live in and maintain ecclesiastical property to discharge their vocation. Current practice but to be replaced by legislation from 6 April 2010 is therefore to exclude from earnings for Class 1 purposes any reimbursements for heating and lighting, and cleaning. In fact, NIM05698 states succinctly:

> It would be very difficult, if not impossible, to establish exactly how the reimbursement of expenses is divided between the business and private use of the accommodation. We therefore exclude from Class 1 NICs any reimbursement of expenses in respect of heating, lighting and cleaning.

However, this principle does not extend to Class 1A contributions, which will be in point where – as may often be the case – the employer has entered into the contracts for these services.

48   National Insurance Fund

Add the following paragraph to the end of the first paragraph in 48.9 on page 630:

Following a review by HM Revenue and Customs, CRND and HM Treasury, a change to the Fund's investment strategy was approved in December 2006 and actioned in January 2007, when all gilt holdings were realised and the proceeds placed into the Debt Management Account Deposit Facility.

51   Overseas Matters

Insert the following sentence in place of the first sentence in the last paragraph 51.4 on page 650:

The ordinary residence indicators at page 7 of the current edition of Leaflet NI 38 give the type of factors which are used currently to decide on ordinary residence.

Insert the following sentence immediately after point (C) on page 657 in 51.8:

For HMRC's view on the definition of immediately see HMRC Press Release on 25 November 2009.

Insert the following sentence immediately before the penultimate sentence in 51.10 on page 664:

For HMRC's view on the definition of immediately see HMRC Press Release on 25 November 2009.

Insert the following paragraph in place of the first paragraph in 51.13 on pages 665 and 666:

For social security purposes (but not necessarily for other purposes) the European Community presently consists of Austria (from 1 January 1995); Belgium; Bulgaria (from 1 January

2007); Cyprus (from 1 May 2004); Czech Republic (from 1 May 2004); Denmark (excluding the Faroe Islands and including Greenland from 1.4.73 to 31.1.85 but not thereafter); Estonia (from 1 May 2004); Finland (from 1 January 1995); France (including Corsica, Guadeloupe, Martinique, Réunion, French Guiana and Saint-Pierre et Miquelon, but excluding Monaco); Germany (consisting of, until 3.10.90, the Federal Republic, ie West Germany and West Berlin but, thereafter, both the former Federal Republic and the former German Democratic Republic); Greece (including Crete and the Greek Islands ie Macedonia, Thrace, Epirus, Thessaly, the Peloponese, the Dodecanese, the Cyclades, the Ionian Islands and the Aegean Islands); Hungary (from 1 May 2004); Ireland; Italy (including Sicily, Sardinia, Trieste and Elba, but excluding Vatican City and San Marino); Latvia (from 1 May 2004); Lithuania (from 1 May 2004); Luxembourg; Malta (from 1 May 2004); the Netherlands (excluding the Netherlands Antilles); Poland (from 1 May 2004); Portugal (including Madeira and the Azores); Romania (from 1 January 2007); Slovakia (from 1 May 2004); Slovenia (from 1 May 2004); Spain (including the Balearic Islands of Majorca, Minorca, Ibiza and Formantara, the Canary Islands and the Spanish enclaves of Ceuta and Melilla in North Africa); Sweden (from 1 January 1995); and the United Kingdom of Great Britain and Northern Ireland (including Gibraltar but excluding the Isle of Man and the Channel Islands). (See HM Revenue and Customs National Insurance Manual NIM33003).

Replace the last two sentences in 51.13 in the third paragraph on page 668 with the following:

The implementation date will be 1 May 2010. It is understood that the UK will not be applying the rules on third country nationals to the new regulations and therefore *EC Reg 1408/71* will continue to apply.

Replace the first paragraph in 51.14 on page 669 with the following:

See also below regarding EC Administrative Decision 181, which extends *Art 14(1)* and *Art 14b(1)* to ensure that there must be a direct relationship between the worker and employer. EC Regulation 1408/71 has been simplified and published as *EC Regulation 883/2004*. *Article 12* of the new Regulation suggests that a person who is being sent abroad must already be in employment in the home country with the employer and must not now be replacing another person as in (b) above. The new regulation will come into force on 1 May 2010 now that the revised Implementing Regulation has been published (the replacement for *EC Regulation 574/72*). This was *EC Regulation 987/2009* published on 30 October 2009. Also published on the same day was *EC Regulation 988/2009* which amends *EC Regulation 883/2004*.

Replace the third paragraph in 51.14 on page 669 with the following:

It is a popular misconception that the certificate E101 is issued only in temporary secondment situations. This is not so. The document certifies continuing Social Security coverage in the 'home' state and is of equal application where work is carried out in more than one EEA state (see **51.15** below). Well over 50,000 E101s are issued each year by HMRC CAR Residency. E101s already in existence when the new general regulations, mentioned above under *EC Regs 883/2004*, come into force are likely continue to their expiry.

Replace the fourth paragraph in 51.15 on page 675 with the following:

Article 14.2(a) will no longer apply under EC Reg 883/2004 from 1 May 2010 (see **51.14**). All multi-state workers will be covered by the same rules.

Replace the last two sentences in the sixth paragraph in 51.15 on page 675 with the following:

The new rules may prevent this. The definition of 'substantial' still has to be determined.

53   Rates and Limits

Replace the Table in 53.15 on page 702 with the following:

From	Overdue contributions	Overpaid contributions
	%	%
29 September 2009	3.0	0.50
24 March 2009	2.5	Zero
27 January 2009	3.5	Zero
6 January 2009	4.5	0.75
6 December 2008	5.5	1.50
6 November 2008	6.5	2.25
6 January 2008	7.5	3.00
6 August 2007	8.5	4.00
6 September 2006	7.5	3.00
6 September 2005	6.5	2.25
6 September 2004	7.5	3.00
6 December 2003	6.5	2.25
6 August 2003	5.5	1.50
6 November 2001	6.5	2.25
6 May 2001	7.5	3.00
6 February 2000	8.5	4.00
6 March 1999	7.5	3.00
6 January 1999	8.5	4.00
6 August 1997	9.5	4.75
31 January 1997	8.5	4.00
6 February 1996	6.25	6.25
6 March 1995	7.0	7.00
6 October 1994	6.25	6.25
6 January 1994	5.5	5.50
6 March 1993	6.25	6.25

57   Subpostmasters

Replace the second paragraph of 57.1 on page 728 with the following:

In all there are three categories of Post Office, numbering in all just over 11,900 offices as at 31 March 2009. The first is Crown Post Offices, of which there were 375 as at 31 March 2009. The second is main post offices of which there are three types (see below). The third is the true sub-Post Office (also known as agency post-offices) – these form the vast majority of the 11,900 offices and of these the majority are governed by a 'Subpostmaster's Contract (1994 version) (R6)'. The second category referred to above comprises franchised main post offices, independent offices within large stores, and modified sub-post offices. Modified sub-post offices are Crown Post Offices which have been put out to contract. Modified subpostmasters are employees of the Post Office.

PRE-BUDGET REPORT PRESS RELEASES RELATING TO NICS

INCOME TAX RATES AND ALLOWANCES

2009 Pre-Budget Report announces that the main rates of income tax for 2010-11 will remain at 20 per cent for basic rate taxpayers and 40 per cent for higher-rate taxpayers. As announced at Budget 2009 an additional rate of tax of 50 per cent will apply on income over £150,000

As announced at the 2008 Pre-Budget Report, tax allowances and thresholds will be frozen in 2010-11 at a time when RPI is negative, with taxpayers receiving a real terms benefit from the maintenance of 2009-10 levels.

This means that the personal allowance for 2010-11 will remain at £6,475 and the age related allowance will remain at £9,490 for people aged between 65 and 74, and to £9,640 for those aged 75 and over. In 2010-11 no one aged 65 or over need pay tax on an income of up to £182 a week.

Income tax allowances

£ per year (unless stated)	2009-10	Change	2010-11
Income tax personal and age-related allowances			
Personal allowance (age under 65)	£6,475	-	£6,475
Personal allowance (age 65-74)	£9,490	-	£9,490
Personal allowance (age 75 and over)	£9,640	-	£9,640
Married couple's allowance* (age 75 and over)	£6,965	-	£6,965
Married couple's allowance* - minimum amount	£2,670	-	£2,670
Income limit for age-related allowances	£22,900	-	£22,900
Blind person's allowance	£1,890	-	£1,890

*Married couple's allowance is given at the rate of 10 per cent

Income tax: taxable bands

2009-10	£ per year	2010-11	£ per year
Starting savings rate: 10%*	£0-£2,440	Starting savings rate: 10%*	£0-£2,440
Basic rate: 20%	£0-£37,400	Basic rate: 20%	£0-£37,400
Higher rate: 40%	Over £37,400	Higher rate: 40%	£37,401-£150,000
Additional rate: 50%		Over £150,000	

* There is a 10p starting rate for savings only. If an individual's non-savings taxable income exceeds the starting rate limit, the 10p starting rate for savings will not be available for savings income.

NATIONAL INSURANCE CONTRIBUTIONS

2009 Pre-Budget Report announces that the starting point for employers', employees' and self employed National Insurance Contributions (NICs) will be maintained at £110 per week despite RPI being negative. The upper earnings and profits limits for Class 1 and Class 4 NICs respectively will also be maintained at their current level of £844 a week, and for the self-employed, the rate of Class 2 contributions will continue to be £2.40 a week. Class 3 contributions will also remain at their current rate of £12.05. In line with the increase in the amount of the state pension, the lower earnings limit and the special class 2 rate for volunteer development workers which are linked to this level will rise to £97 a week and £4.85 a week respectively.

National insurance contributions

£ per week (unless stated)	2009-10	Change	2010-11
Lower earnings limit, primary Class 1	£95	£2	£97
Upper earnings limit, primary Class 1	£844	-	£844
Upper Accruals Point	£770	-	£770
Primary threshold	£110	-	£110
Secondary threshold	£110	-	£110
Employees' primary Class 1 rate between primary threshold and upper earnings limit	11%	-	11%
Employees' primary Class 1 rate above upper earnings limit	1%	-	1%
Employees' contracted-out rebate - salary-related schemes	1.6%	-	1.6%
Employees' contracted-out rebate - money-purchase schemes	1.6%	-	1.6%
Married women's reduced rate between primary threshold and upper earnings limit	4.85%	-	4.85%
Married women's rate above upper earnings limit	1%	-	1%
Employers' secondary Class 1 rate above secondary threshold	12.8%	-	12.8%
Employers' contracted-out rebate, salary-related schemes	3.7%	-	3.7%
Employers' contracted-out rebate, money-purchase schemes	1.4%	-	1.4%
Class 2 rate	£2.40	-	£2.40

Pre-Budget Report Press Releases

£ per week (unless stated)	2009-10	Change	2010-11
Class 2 small earnings exception (per year)	£5,075	-	£5,075
Special Class 2 rate for share fishermen	£3.05	-	£3.05
Special Class 2 rate for volunteer development workers	£4.75	£0.10	£4.85
Class 3 rate (per week)	£12.05	-	£12.05
Class 4 lower profits limit (per year)	£5,715	-	£5,715
Class 4 upper profits limit (per year)	£43,875	-	£43,875
Class 4 rate between lower profits limit and upper profits limit	8%	-	8%
Class 4 rate above upper profits limit	1%	-	1%

National Insurance Contributions

The Pre-Budget Report announces that the employee, employer and self-employed rates o
National Insurance Contributions (NICs) will increase by 0.5 per cent in April 2011 i
addition to the 0.5% increase announced at the 2008 Pre-Budget Report.

To ensure that the lowest earners are protected from the rise in NICs rates, the level at whic
people start to pay NICs will increase in April 2011 by £570 above the level previousl
announced. Those paying the standard employee rate and earning under £20,000 will pay les
NICs overall as result of these changes.

Personal Tax

The Government has today announced that as part of the package to support sound publi
finances, the point at which individuals start to pay the higher rate of income tax , known as th
higher rate threshold, will be maintained in 2012/13 at 2011/12 levels. The upper earning
limit and the upper profits limit for national insurance will continue to be aligned with th
higher rate threshold. To ensure that those on low incomes do not lose out the persona
allowance will be indexed in line with inflation in 2012/13.

PBRN1: NATIONAL INSURANCE CONTRIBUTIONS RATES AND THRESHOLDS

Who is likely to be affected?

1.   All employers, employees and the self employed.

General description of the measure

2.   This measure sets the National Insurance Contributions (NICs) rates and threshold
that will apply for 2010-11. The Lower Earnings Limit (LEL) which is linked to th
basic State Pension will increase by £2 to £97 per week and the special Class 2 rate fo
Volunteer Development Workers will increase by 10p to £4.85 per week as this i
linked to the LEL. All other NICs rates and thresholds are unchanged for 2010-11.

3.   The 2008 Pre-Budget Report (PBR) announced that from 2011-12 the main rate o
Class 1 and Class 4 NICs will be increased by 0.5 per cent to 11.5 per cent and 8.5 pe

cent respectively. The Class 1 employer rate will be increased by 0.5 per cent to 13.3 per cent. The increased rate will apply to Class 1A and 1B contributions. The additional rate of Class 1 and 4 NICs will also be increased by 0.5 per cent to 1.5 per cent.

4. From 2011-12, this measure increases the main rate of Class 1 and 4 NICs by a further 0.5 per cent to 12 per cent and 9 per cent respectively.

5. The Class 1 employer rate will be increased by a further 0.5 per cent to 13.8 per cent from 2011-12. The increased rate will also apply to Class 1A and 1B contributions.

6. The additional rate of Class 1 and 4 NICs will be increased by a further 0.5 per cent to 2 per cent from 2011-12.

7. The primary threshold and lower profits limit will be increased by £570 for 2011-12 above plans announced in the 2008 PBR to compensate the lowest earners for the increase in the Class 1 and 4 rates.

Operative date

8. The increase in the NICs LEL and the special rate for Volunteer Development Workers will have effect on and after 6 April 2010.

9. The changes to the NICs primary threshold and the rates of NICs will have effect on and after 6 April 2011.

Current law and proposed revisions

10. The change to the LEL for 2010-11 will be introduced by regulations.

11. The change to the rates of Class 1 and 4 NICs in 2011-12 will require a National Insurance Contributions Bill.

Further advice

12. If you have any questions about this change, please contact Hasan Mustafa on 020 7147 2508 (email: hasan.mustafa@hmrc.gsi.gov.uk). Information about Pre-Budget Report measures is available on the HM Revenue & Customs website at www.hmrc.gov.uk.

PBRN25: SALARY SACRIFICE: RESTRICTING THE TAX EXEMPTION FOR WORKPLACE CANTEENS

Who is likely to be affected?

1. Employers and employees who have structured contractual remuneration arrangements, involving salary sacrifice or flexible benefits, that are intended to allow employees to obtain meals at work partly or wholly free of liability to tax and National Insurance Contributions (NICs).

General description of the measure

2. Section 317 of the Income Tax (Earnings and Pensions) Act 2003 (ITEPA) provides an exemption from tax under the employment income rules whereby an employer can provide the benefit of free or subsidised meals in a canteen or on its business premises, subject to certain conditions.

3. The Government has become aware that some employers and employees have developed remuneration arrangements involving salary sacrifice or flexible benefits to take advantage of this exemption.

4. These arrangements are intended to allow some employees to purchase meals out of gross pay, and hence obtain a significant tax and NICs advantage over the majority of

employees who must purchase their meals using their net pay, from which tax and NICs have already been deducted.

5. Legislation will be introduced in Finance Bill 2010 to amend section 317 of ITEPA to restrict the exemption for the benefit of free or subsidised meals where an employee has an entitlement in conjunction with salary sacrifice or flexible benefits arrangements to employer-provided free or subsidised meals.

Operative date

6. The measure will have effect on and after 6 April 2011.

Current law and proposed revisions

7. Section 317 of ITEPA removes the tax charge on the provision of meals for directors or employees if the meal is provided in a canteen or on the employer's premises and the following conditions are met: • the meal is on a reasonable scale; • all employees, or all employees at a particular work location, may obtain a free or subsidised meal (or a voucher for one); and • in the case of a hotel, catering or similar business, if free or subsidised meals are provided for employees in a restaurant or dining room when meals are being served to the public, part of the dining area must be designated for staff use only and the meals must be taken in that part.

8. The proposed revisions will remove the tax exemption in circumstances where employees are in effect using a designated amount of their gross remuneration to fund the purchase of food and drink at work.

9. The measure will achieve this by amending section 317 of ITEPA to restrict its application.

10. Firstly, the amendment will prevent the exemption from applying where the provision of free or subsidised meals is linked to a salary sacrifice arrangement in which the employee has agreed to reduce their existing taxable employment income and is to be provided with food and drink (or the means of obtaining it) of a value that is commensurate with the amount of income given up.

11. Secondly, the amendment will prevent the exemption from applying where the provision of free or subsidised meals is linked to a flexible benefits remuneration arrangement which includes the provision of food and drink (or the means of obtaining food and drink) of a value that is commensurate with the amount of income given up.

12. The rules on employment-related benefits will apply in the normal way to the provision of food and drink to which the restriction in the exemption applies. Similarly, Class 1A employer NIC liability will apply in the normal way.

13. The section 317 exemption will continue to apply in relation to general subsidies for canteens that are available to all employees, for example where the employer provides a general subsidy that is reflected in lower prices in the canteen.

14. The existing position in relation to subsidy benefits that are quantifiable but not connected to salary sacrifice or flexible benefits arrangements will not be affected.

15. The Luncheon Voucher exemption for the first 15p for each working day will not be affected.

16. The existing rules will continue to apply to the tax/NICs treatment of other meals at work and working lunches.

17. Arrangements that apportion employment income to meals at work in such a way that it ranks as earnings will be liable to tax and Class 1 NICs under Pay As You Earn as earnings, as has always been the case.

Further advice

18. Draft legislation and an explanatory note for this measure will be published on the HM Revenue & Customs website in the New Year.

19. If you have any questions about this change, please contact David McDowell on 020 7147 0175 (email: david.mcdowell@hmrc.gsi.gov.uk). Information about Pre-Budget Report measures is available on the HM Revenue & Customs website at www.hmrc.gov.uk

PBRN26: CHANGES TO COMPANY CAR TAX

Who is likely to be affected?

1. Employees provided with a company car that is available for their private use and employers who bear Class 1A National Insurance Contributions (NICs) on the taxable benefit of company cars.

General description of the measure

2. Legislation will be introduced in Finance Bill 2010 to set the company car tax charge for 2012-13.

Operative date

3. The measure will have effect on and after 6 April 2012.

Current law and proposed revisions

4. Section 139 of the Income Tax (Earnings and Pensions) Act 2003 sets out the basis for calculating the appropriate percentage for cars with CO_2 emissions. The appropriate percentage multiplied by the list price of the car (adjusted for any taxable accessories) provides the level of chargeable benefit for company car tax and Class 1A NICs.

5. The current graduated table of company car tax bands will be extended down to a new 10 per cent band, and all CO_2 emissions thresholds moved down by 5g/km on 6 April 2012 so that the 10 per cent band will apply to company cars with CO_2 emissions up to 99g/km. Qualifying Low Emissions Cars (QUALECs) will therefore no longer exist as a separate category.

Further advice

6. If you have any questions about this change, please contact the Employer Helpline on 0845 7143 143 or your local HMRC Enquiry Centre. Information about Pre-Budget Report measures is available on the HM Revenue & Customs website at www.hmrc.gov.uk

PBRN27: COMPANY CAR TAX: ELECTRIC CARS

Who is likely to be affected?

1. Employees and directors who are provided for their private use with a company car propelled solely by electricity and employers who bear Class 1A National Insurance Contributions (NICs) on the taxable benefit of company cars.

General description of the measure

2. Legislation will be introduced in 2010 to reduce the appropriate percentage to 0 per cent for electric cars for the purposes of company car tax. This reduces the car benefit charge for electric cars to nil.

Pre-Budget Report Press Releases

Operative date

3.   The measure will have effect on and after 6 April 2010 for five years.

Current law and proposed revisions

4.   Section 140(3)(a) of the Income Tax (Earnings and Pensions) Act 2003 sets out the basis for calculating the appropriate percentage for cars which are wholly electrically propelled.

5.   The current appropriate percentage of 9 per cent will be reduced to 0 per cent with effect from 6 April 2010, and will apply for five years.

Further advice

6.   If you have any questions about this change, please contact the Employer Helpline on 0845 7143 143 or your local HMRC Enquiry Centre. Information about Pre-Budget Report measures is available on the HM Revenue & Customs website at www.hmrc.gov.uk

PBRN28: VAN BENEFIT CHARGE: ELECTRIC VANS

Who is likely to be affected?

1.   Employees and directors who are provided for their private use with a van propelled solely by electricity and employers who bear Class 1A National Insurance Contributions (NICs) on the taxable benefit of company vans.

General description of the measure

2.   Legislation will be introduced in Finance Bill 2010 to set a new, lower flat rate benefit charge for electric vans for the purposes of the van benefit charge. The rate will be set at nil for electric vans.

Operative date

3.   The measure will have effect on and after 6 April 2010 for five years.

Current law and proposed revisions

4.   The basis for calculating the van benefit charge is set out in sections 154-159 of the Income Tax (Earnings and Pensions) Act 2003.

5.   The current flat rate of £3,000 for all vans will be reduced to nil for electric vans with effect from 6 April 2010, and will apply for five years.

6.   The van benefit legislation will be amended to include a definition of an electric van for this purpose.

Further advice

7.   If you have any questions about this change, please contact the Employer Helpline on 0845 7143 143 or your local HMRC Enquiry Centre. Information about Pre-Budget Report measures is available on the HM Revenue & Customs website at www.hmrc.gov.uk

PBRN29: CARS AND VANS: CHANGES TO FUEL BENEFIT TAX

Who is likely to be affected?

1.   Employees who receive free private fuel from their employers for company cars or vans and employers who bear Class 1A National Insurance Contributions (NICs) on the taxable benefit of provided fuel.

General description of the measure

2. The measure sets the fuel benefit charge for company cars and vans from 2010-11.

Operative date

3. The measure will have effect on and after 6 April 2010.

Current law and proposed revisions

4. Section 150(1) of the Income Tax (Earnings and Pensions) Act 2003 (ITEPA) provides the figure to be used as the basis for calculating the benefit of private fuel received for a company car which is chargeable to tax and Class 1A NICs. This figure is currently set at £16,900 and will be increased to £18,000.

5. Similarly, section 161 of ITEPA provides the figure to be used as the basis for calculating the benefit of private fuel received for a company van which is chargeable to tax and Class 1A NICs. This figure is currently set at £500 and will be increased to £550.

Further advice

6. If you have any questions about this change, please contact the Employer Helpline on 0845 7143 143 or your local HMRC Enquiry Centre. Information about Pre-Budget Report measures is available on the HM Revenue & Customs website at www.hmrc.gov.uk

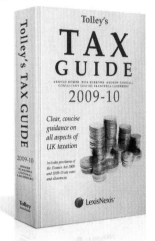

Cutting back isn't always good for you

We understand that in the current economic climate there is more pressure than ever to work cost-effectively; but you still need to be confident that you are complying with the latest tax legislation or providing clients with the most accurate advice you can.

Tolley's Tax Guide 2009-10 deciphers complex tax legislation into straightforward English; a time-saving reference source when supplying tax solutions for your clients.

The first point of reference for tax practitioners, this essential title has the latest tax rates and allowances, worked examples and practical tax points so you can understand where, when and how the rules apply. Covering the major UK taxes, the 45 chapters of Tolley's Tax Guide are split into 8 sections for ease of use and reference and include outline of the UK tax system, employment, pensions, trades, professions and vocations, land and buildings, tax and the family, choosing your investment and other areas, including trusts and estates and the overseas situation.

"Never has such a book been so necessary as this year."
Tina Riches, Technical Director, CIOT

Purchase this title today!

Visit www.lexisnexis.co.uk/tax or call
0845 370 1234 quoting AD9559